Prepping

I0421546

The Ultimate Beginner's Guide to Prepping, Survivalism and Bug Out Bags For When SHTF

Table Of Contents

Introduction

This short book aims to give you valuable information about the various components involved in formulating a good, flexible, handy and resourceful survival plan for when SHTF.

SHTF stands for *Shit Hits The Fan* – referring to any circumstance or condition that disrupts life, as you know it to be. It is when something so devastating happens that you cannot return to the way you normally lived your life. When you understand the importance of prepping, then there is a good probability that you will start your own preparation plans.

Preparation is vital to survival. Knowing why and how you should prepare will be key factors in ensuring your safety and security during difficult or calamitous circumstances. Understanding your environment and being aware of what is going on around you will further help you to recognize the skills and supplies that will be necessary to keep you and your family alive.

This short, concise book aims to help you in your journey of preparing! Hopefully you can learn a few things from it.

Chapter 1:

What is Prepping?

With the comfortable living environment that most people experience today, especially in the Western World, it is hard to convince the average person that something terrible could happen to life, as we know it. People tend to find it hard to conjure up images of horrific situations, and they may even think it's impossible to experience life any other way. With this mindset, these people are not likely to take steps to prepare for such eventualities or to ensure both safety and survival.

Unfortunately, history tells us otherwise. Take the Pearl Harbor bombing for example, or Hurricane Katrina. Lots of lives were lost, which could have been avoided if necessary precautions were taken. While we should not be pessimistic and always assume that the worst things will happen to us, it is sensible and wise to at least prepare for the worst.

Additionally, preparation is not only limited to conditions resulting in war or natural calamities. We can also prep ourselves for economic fallouts or even alien invasions and zombies. More common behavior is prepping for something simple and ordinary, such as a power failure or regional drought. Yet, when a natural disaster, such as a hurricane, tornado, drought or flooding, does take place, the majority of people are, unfortunately, not prepared to handle these conditions.

Some events that require adequate preparation include the following:

Earthquakes

Fires

Floods

Hurricanes

Tornadoes

Tsunamis

Mass Shootings

Invasions

Riots

Robbery

Declaration of Martial Law

Acts of Terrorism

Epidemics or Breakouts

Those who are experienced preppers understand that they may not know what will happen in the future, but they can still always prepare. The best prepping involves items that are part of one's everyday life. Having a first aid kit with you, jumper cables in your car, stock of emergency food and the likes are essentially helpful.

They are readily available for your everyday use as well as in case of a disaster. A successful prepper is usually one that is constantly on the lookout for valuable items that will help him/her today *and* when emergency strikes.

The idea of proactively prepping has been practiced throughout history and is even seen in the natural world, whether it is a squirrel collecting nuts for the long-term or a coastal city consistently improving their levee system. During times like the Great Depression, many people stored weeks, and even months, worth of food in their pantry. This behavior is contrary to what most people practice in our current society

- only purchasing enough food for a few weeks and leaving it in the fridge so it does not spoil.

Prepping is not just about preparing your assets – food, water, medicine, weapons, etc. – for survival. It is also about preparing your body and your mind. You need to be aware of what is happening around you. This will help you identify potential threats to your safety and security so that you can avoid them and know how to deal with them if and when the time comes.

A good way to prepare your mind is to learn skills that are useful for a number of emergency situations and calamities. It is also helpful to learn practical martial arts so that you know what to do in order to avoid being mugged if attacked. This will help you be aware of what is going on around you so you can steer clear of danger.

To prepare your body is just as important. You need to be in good shape and in optimal health if you desire to survive through adverse circumstances. In the event of a disaster or an unexpected unfortunate event, you want to be able to outrun or elude and outlive threats.

Good mind preparation involves knowing that you cannot control everything that happens in your life. It is good to recognize that you have no way of knowing what might happen. This will keep your mind sharp in regards to prepping your physical assets. For example, you can always carry around a pepper spray or a small pocketknife in your bag or have a handy toolkit or first aid box in your car. To have an idea of what to prep for, your mindset can start with, "If something happens when _____ or at _____, I should have/do _____."

Another important concept of a good plan is to recognize that you cannot control when a disaster strikes. Get into the habit of thinking, "What if something happened while you were

_____?" That blank could be "at work" or any of the other places you frequently go to.

Start with the Everyday Carry

To help you get into the habit of prepping, you can start with the simplest prepping method - having an everyday carry (EDC). It is a small bag that contains vital items that you carry every day and everywhere you go. Some basic items in an everyday carry could be the following:

First Aid Kit

Pocket Knife

Flashlight

Extra Clothes

Water Packets

Food Rations

When preparing an EDC bag, you should attempt to think of everything that would come in handy for your survival if you could not get back home for the next twenty-four hours.

Prepping is all about being practical and self-sufficient. It teaches you to rely less on what is available in the world for your convenience, such as electricity. When you learn basic survival skills and you have basic survival possessions, you will not feel as great of an impact as others may when outside utilities are not available to you anymore.

It is important to start preparing your mind, your body and your possessions early because prepping for survival does not come easy, and it does not happen overnight. You need to understand the steps to take when a range of disasters or calamities happen. You can start to prepare your body for limited food and water consumption even before the need for it arrives. You can study how to collect water and sanitize it so that you can use it to drink. Also, you can try to look for alternative supplies of energy, should existing power resources fail.

Chapter 2:

History of Prepping and Survivalism

Survivalism is about preparing for any kind of emergency, such as natural calamities or catastrophes, social upheavals, political disorders, economic fallouts, and the likes. It is about getting yourself ready to face whatever happens when life, as you know it, goes into turmoil.

Survivalism involves becoming self-sufficient – being able to build important structures to ensure your safety and security, knowing how to obtain food and water sources, stocking up the same for immediate survival, and training for and possessing the necessary life skills to defend one's self and family.

The beginnings of survivalism can be traced back to the 1950s when there were threats of economic collapse, social disturbances, atomic and nuclear wars, government procedure and even apocalyptic religious beliefs. People prepared personal shelters and food supplies.

Proponents of survivalism allude to the effects of the Great Depression as a good case in point. Many other crises followed this time period, such as the oil crises, wars, famine, inflation and energy shortages. People built fallout shelters in their homes and increased security. Some even opted for ballistic defense, while others just prepared stockpiles of food, water, and other supplies for their household.

Survivalists were also referred to as retreaters. People would leave their homes or cities and go to remote places that would serve as a refuge. People preferred to avoid conflicts and become invisible, instead of fighting off the threats. This is where survivalism was more defined, as it really meant something that was combative, doing everything necessary in order to survive.

Because the general public expected bad years and bad situations to come, survivalists promoted the concept of survivalism all the more. Publications, seminars and retreats were done to make the public more aware of the need for a change in lifestyle.

One such boost in promoting survivalism consciousness was when the fear of the Y2K bug hit at the close of 1999. People became afraid of potential disasters and fallouts. While there were minimal consequences of the computer bug, people became interested in survivalism and prepping after the September 11th bombing in the United States, as well as in other areas.

The devastating effects of many natural calamities, such as floods, earthquakes, hurricanes, and tsunamis, all over the world only added to this interest. People feared that the changing climate and environmental disasters could no longer be avoided – they would inevitably come at one time or another. War, terrorism and sickness were bound to catch up to unknowing victims and the economy became uncertain.

Prepping became a chief concern, and it was more than having enough supplies to last. People also wanted to be skilled to survive and be in contact with people who thought like they did. With the rise of social media on the Internet, the message of prepping was then seen by people who had previously been unaware of the philosophy. Moreover, it was then seen that survivalism was not just about riding out the storm by yourself. Instead, people came to realize that communalism is vital and that working together was the best way to go about difficult situations.

Chapter 3:

The Science Behind Prepping

Prepping is a discipline. It is a science and art of acquiring and implementing knowledge, knowing what to do before and during a devastating event starts by thinking about and writing out one's gameplan. The best preppers are able to find a way to help other people prepare, especially their family and friends. Here are some things that will help you understand the discipline of prepping:

Creating a Bug Out and Bug In Plan

Understand what you need to do when circumstances dictate that you should leave your home. If you are going to evacuate, where is this place and how will you go there? How will you even get out of your home when evil forces or barricades surround you? How will you get away from devastations, such as tornadoes, typhoons, floods, etc.? What do you need to pack that will help sustain your life while you are out?

If you are bugging in, for example, when power goes out and you can only stay put, do you have everything handy? Are you going to be comfortable while you stay in? When you are caved in and cannot go out, do you have an ample stock of food and water? Is there a way you can communicate with the outside world?

Prepping for bugging in and bugging out go hand in hand - you can either settle down or move out. However, the two plans will always entail stocking up for survival and building up your defenses.

Creating a Communications Plan

Emergencies will require you to communicate. Isolating yourself for extended periods of time can rarely ever be a long-term solution. No matter how well stocked you are, you will have to contact other people at some point to know the current situation, to know where they are, to ask for help or to give help. Communication will help you plan and coordinate your direction and your moves.

Building Teams

Survival is best when people work together. Sure you can do it alone but you have to expect that people will still come to you and ask for your help because they did not prepare, so you might as well build a team and prepare them.

Another aspect that you want to consider is that the people who will naturally come to you for help are your neighbors. If you face an event that is not indefinite, then you will still be neighbors with them, so it is good to help them anyway.

Preparing your family is very important. However, they can't be relying on just you for their survival. Teach them how to survive as an individual and assign tasks that they can do. Buy extra supplies and equipment that they can use.

If your family lives far from you and a disaster comes, then they might just show up at your doorstep unless otherwise instructed. Be prepared for this.

Create a Training Plan

Learn basic and critical survival skills and study how to teach them to others. When you run out of supplies or items, skills will be very valuable. You need to adapt to your situation and make the most of what is available at all times. Hunting skills, making fires, medical skills, foraging, building, sourcing and filtering water, and making weapons are some of the skills that are quite useful for survival.

Learn how to improvise. Be patient with teaching your team about these skills so that you will not be the only person to do all the tasks. When you learn and prepare yourself for any type of incident, you will not have a hard time adjusting in dire situations. Practice your skills often so that you and your loved ones are confident in your abilities to protect yourselves and each other.

Make sure that your supplies and equipment are up-to-date. What's the use of a big stock of supplies (like food and medicine) that are expired or equipment (like vehicles and weapons) that do not function? Regularly check everything that is critical. This way, you can also recognize if there is something that you do not need to bring.

It is also important to check your progress on a consistent basis. Are you building your supplies well? Are you building your teams well? The process of prepping sounds easy, but it entails a lot of work. Again, you need to remember that understanding the how-tos and the whys behind prepping will ensure survival, even in the most awful conditions.

Chapter 4:

The Effects of Prepping A Bug Out Bag

The idea of preparing the Bug Out Bag (BOB) sounds easy enough. It is about putting important survival possessions in one bag so that you can grab it and go when disaster strikes or when SHTF.

The question then becomes, do we *really* need a BOB? Remember the saying, "Chance always smiles upon the prepared." It is better to be ready than to be sorry when a bad situation arises and causes you to flee and struggle to survive. So, there is no harm in preparation.

Perhaps the biggest benefit of having a BOB is that it will give you a sense of security and peace. You will be confident that you can face anything because you are well equipped.

A BOB can be prepared in many ways. You can even get these bags fully equipped online or in stores, as many of these bags are mass-produced. However, if you want variety, then you can tailor fit your BOB according to your needs and living environment. If this is your goal, then you can pack a specific BOB for yourself or for your family.

Whatever your personal requirements and variables are, there are certain basic rules that apply to most people in regards to the contents of their BOB:

You should be able to carry your BOB with ease. Survival may require you to go a far distance or through various landscapes. If your bag is too heavy, then you will find it hard to move around.

Remember that your BOB is for survival and not designed to be a mobile home. Come up with a simple list of necessary and reliable items – things that you really need to survive.

The concept of BOB contents is to help you become self-sufficient. Ideally, you want items that complement each other and can also stand on their own.

When prepping your items list, you should think of a target time period. For example, a BOB can be expected to last for 24 hours, 72 hours or for seven days.

Bug Out Bags are for survival, and they are not for comfort or luxury. This thought will help you prepare a BOB that is essential and not too heavy.

Now that you have a good understanding of the purpose of your BOB, here is a list of basic items you can consider putting inside the bag:

Water

Remember, you can only last three days without potable water.

Food essentials

You can pack energy bars so that you have lightweight food packed with calories.

Compass

This will help you with navigation if there is no electricity.

Map

This will help you with directions and identifying landscape and landmarks.

Paracord

This is useful for many things, especially for making a temporary shelter.

Tarp

A small tarp can be rolled into your bag to provide needed shelter, and it can also be used to signal for help.

Magnesium Fire Starter

You never know when you need fire to make a light or to prepare a meal.

Socks

Packing spare clothes is good, but socks are on top of a clothing priority list. Use a synthetic blend or wool for more comfort and protection for your feet.

Survival blanket

This is better than a sleeping bag because of its versatility and durability.

Flashlight

It is better to utilize a LED flashlight than older, traditional bulbs.

Radio

Hand cranked radios will prove more useful than mobile phones. You can get important information on what is occurring around you.

Needless to say, each person's BOB will be different from another's, depending on their location, basic needs, length of expected survival needs, and the number of people he/she will go with. It is also important to choose the ideal bag that can contain these essentials in a way that is comfortable to carry for potentially extended periods of time.

It is important to remember that preparation does not stop after one completes their BOB. One must check its contents periodically to see if all the items are still useful and working, especially in regards to batteries. Also, make note of all the expiration dates.

To prepare even further, you can check out what other people's Bug Out Bags contain. They may foresee something that you overlooked or didn't prioritize. Reading blogs or checking out YouTube videos are great options when wanting to know what others use.

Chapter 5:

Pros and Cons of Prepping

Some people present the idea that prepping is a waste of time if disaster doesn't strike. However, they will be surprised to know that prepping has its advantages, whether or not something bad comes up and disrupts one's life.

You will stay fit and healthy.

Prepping may involve strengthening your fort, building a more secure home, stocking up on supplies of wood and water, etc. By engaging in these activities regularly, you are actually exercising and making your body fit and healthy.

It saves you money.

If you stock up on supplies, especially when items are on sale, you will have saved a lot on future purchases. Additionally, you will begin to limit your consumption habits and be more conscious when making purchases by determining the long-term value and usability.

You can avoid wastage.

When you keep something because it might be useful in the future, you are being smart. When the time comes that you do actually need it, it will become handy. Prepping helps you avoid throwing otherwise valuable things away and falling into the trap of continuously running through low quality products instead of high quality products that will last.

You avoid inflation.

Because you stock up on everyday supplies, you do not have to worry about blown-up prices during inflation. It is common knowledge within the prepper community that trying to find necessities during a time of disaster is very difficult.

Even if you find those necessities, they are usually way overpriced because of the dramatically increased demand. By buying ahead of time, you are able to avoid not getting what you need or being a victim to inflation.

You are ready for natural disasters even if they don't come, and this gives you a feeling of security.

Part of prepping is securing important documents. This means that when natural disasters, fires or floods happen, you know that you will not suffer loss.

Regular power outages won't be as difficult for you.

You understand evacuation procedures, and you have everything ready for when you need to leave your home.

When you encounter vehicular concerns, such as your car breaking down, you have supplies ready.

When you suffer minor or major financial emergencies, you do not feel stressed. You will have a way of getting by. In the same manner, when you suffer other security concerns, such as losing your job, underemployment or health problems, you know that what you have prepared will come in very handy until you begin to rise above the situation again.

In simple situations, such as stores closing down early, you will have a ready provision of food and other household supplies.

Prepping helps you learn independence. When you are ready to face anything, you will not fear or stress out nearly as much, and you will not have to go to your friend for help because you know that you can handle the situation and survive. On the other hand, you can be the one who helps your friends or family members during these situations.

Not only does prepping make you independent but it also allows you to develop confidence. The thought that you can survive and be okay will help you feel positive during situations in which others around you might be panicking.

Another great advantage of prepping is that it helps families grow closer. By preparing together and learning how to work as a team, they will bond and trust each other on a deeper level.

Chapter 6:

Skills Compared to Stuff

Most people who have the survivalism mindset will think about things that they need to prepare and keep in their Bug Out Bags. While gathering necessary supplies is a good thing to do, there is also another important road that you should take - acquiring skills that will help you get the stuff that you need.

Why is it essential to learn survival skills? Well, if you run out of stuff and the devastating situation is indefinite, you will no longer have any means to survive. Moreover, having the skills to make or produce stuff for survival will lessen your burden of purchasing, storing, and maintaining your supply bag. You will be ready to face life-changing challenges by adapting to your present environment, and you can even use what you have on hand for other purposes.

If you are a prepper, both stuff and skills are essential. Undoubtedly, it is important to stock up on valuable supplies. However, if you were to choose one over the other, skills should hold more weight. When you can't buy something, you can learn to manufacture or put something together for the same purpose.

Here are a few examples of supplies that you can learn to fabricate or substitute, so when a situation arises in which you do not have it in stock or you cannot purchase it, you will still have ample supply.

Medicine

Study how to use available medicine for a variety of uses. For example, some veterinary medicines can be used for other human purposes. Additionally, you can use natural herbs and plants to create poultices as alternative to pills and ointments. You can also use pieces of clothing if you do not have a supply of bandages.

Hunting Gear

Become skilled in regards to how to hunt, skin, and store animals as food. When you run out of food rations in your bag and your situation is indefinite, you should be able to track down and have animals that you can use for food.

While you don't need to be a hunting expert, it is essential to be capable. Furthermore, you can use animals for purposes other than food, such as clothing, shelter, weapons, etc.

Homesteading or growing your own food

While it is certainly helpful to know how to hunt animals, it is arguably even better if you can grow your own food. On top of learning how to store hunted animals as a food source, you can own your own animals and eat them as well.

The same goes for farming edible plants and vegetables. Instead of foraging supplies everyday, grow some crops near you so that you can save energy and ensure adequate provision.

Alcohol

Alcohol can be used for fuel and to help your body cope with difficult climates.

Another important skill to master is self-defense. It is good to be able to master techniques on how to get food and water supplies or build shelters. However, it is also vital that you can protect yourself from danger.

You can learn how to make ammunition, shoot, and fight using sticks or clubs. You should also learn how to communicate with your group in situations that will require you to engage in combat for survival.

Knowing basic survival skills is a big, *big* plus to prepping. Here are some areas that are very important that you can get started on now:

Starting a fire without using matches. You need to know how to utilize friction and some supplies of wood to create a fire for heat, light, cooking and protection from predators.

Tie knots and learn to use vines and ropes.

Build a shelter out of various materials.

Finding and filtering, or sanitizing, water for drinking.

Signaling for SOS.

Getting energy out of a lemon, some copper wires and a piece of nail (when your battery runs out).

Solar cooking

It is good to know these things in your head or even study them through books, shows and other resources. However, to really prepare you for the real thing, you need to go out, probably into the woods, and actually develop these skills. Theory is important, but practice is better. More importantly, knowledge that is not applied is useless.

One more skill to master is the use of electronic devices for communication. Learning to use a ham radio can be very beneficial, especially when mobile phone lines are cut off.

Undoubtedly, there is a multitude of skills to learn when it comes to survival, and the key is to start now. Like they say, you can't learn how to swim when you are already drowning.

Preparation time is never wasted time. Some people think that it is useless, especially when they haven't faced any form of danger in the last ten years. Do not say that you have learned these survival skills for nothing. You never know when they will come in handy. Being adaptable is essential if you want to ensure your survival in the present and in the future.

Learn skills that can help you now and that can be vital in future situations. Even if you die and nothing has happened, it doesn't matter - at least you were ready for anything.

Chapter 7:

The Future of Prepping

Through the years, people have become more and more oriented towards being prepared for safety and to survive in the wilderness. Really, this should be the common case because life-threatening incidents can happen anytime, anywhere, and to anyone.

Survivalism has evolved from simply storing basic supplies to danger awareness, self-defense and personal protection. Scenarios like global warming, asteroid strikes, massive scale of nuclear or biochemical propagation, fatal diseases (like anthrax, ebola, sarin, SARS, dengue, to name a few), and population explosion leading to a variety of health and supply problems can also be considered.

While technology and survival methods may change, basic needs do not. When preparing for survival, you need to understand the basic needs that you have to meet. When you are fully prepared, your mind will be stable and focused. This will keep you from panicking when you are faced with emergency survival situations.

At a base level, the future of humans will still be dependent on basic needs. Your body naturally needs food, water, and air. Fire or shelter may also be a necessity, especially from freezing temperatures, external threats and other natural elements that may be harmful. Here is a description of each necessity, in order of priority, and how you can prepare an adequate supply for the future:

Air

It is said that a human can only survive without air for three minutes. Fresh air is so important to the body and in several extreme cases, such as a chemical explosion, wildfire or nuclear fallout, the air will become toxic and dangerous.

You can prepare gas masks, oxygen tanks, air scrubbers or any kind of air filter to help you get enough clean oxygen when you are in an affected area. Should the previously mentioned incidents happen, though, it is best to evacuate to a safe area.

Water

You can last without water for only three days. The body needs about two liters of water every day, and not just any water will do – you need fresh and potable water to drink. Water in surrounding areas can be contaminated with bacteria, chemicals and other toxins.

This is why you need to learn how to get water from various sources. If there is an available water supply but it is not fresh or potable, then you can still die of dehydration. You need to know how to filter and sanitize water so that you can drink and use it to cook.

Food

You can last without food for a week or so as long, as you have water and your body is fit and healthy. The body naturally stores fat reserves that sustain it during survival mode. Nevertheless, a lack of food may affect your ability to think well and move around because you do not have enough energy.

Learning how to forage food from any kind of environment will be very helpful in survival situations. You should also prepare a food stock that will be handy in emergency cases.

Fire/Shelter

When you find yourself trapped in a cold place or somewhere freezing, you will need fire to survive. You also need a place where you can stay safe from nature and predators. You should learn how to construct shades, or any form of protective space, for your security from any kind of material in any environment you may find yourself in.

Survival training will help you live even though you suffer shipwrecks and similar incidents. It is important to learn how to live through hunger, thirst, stress, various climates and fears as well as brief, prolonged or indefinite natural disasters.

Survival awareness will continue to spread, as interest over prepping will develop over the years. As we live in an era of uncertainty, where so many unfortunate and destructive things are happening around the world, people will learn to prepare all the more. New techniques will be discovered and new skills will be developed. Survival will always be a primary concern of man.

Conclusion

I hope you were able to learn a few things from this book.

In the current world we live in, there are many potential events that can alter the way you live life. It can either bring a good change or it can throw us off balance. There are two options: to ignore potential threats and just wish that life will turn out better soon enough, or prepare ahead for what could happen.

Survivalism is not limited to a select few. Anyone can prepare as long as one puts his/her mind and heart into it. When emergency situations arise, or when shit hits the fan, you have no safety net. You will get affected one way or another. A good way to shield yourself and your family from the devastating effects of a disaster is to be prepared.

You have a choice to make, and you can make that choice as early as now. Just don't wait until it's too late!